NATIVE AMERICAN ARTWORK

www.gaylesfineartworks.com

By Gayle Bariff-Daufel

Inks and Bindings
888-290-5218
www.inksandbindings.com
orders@inksandbindings.com

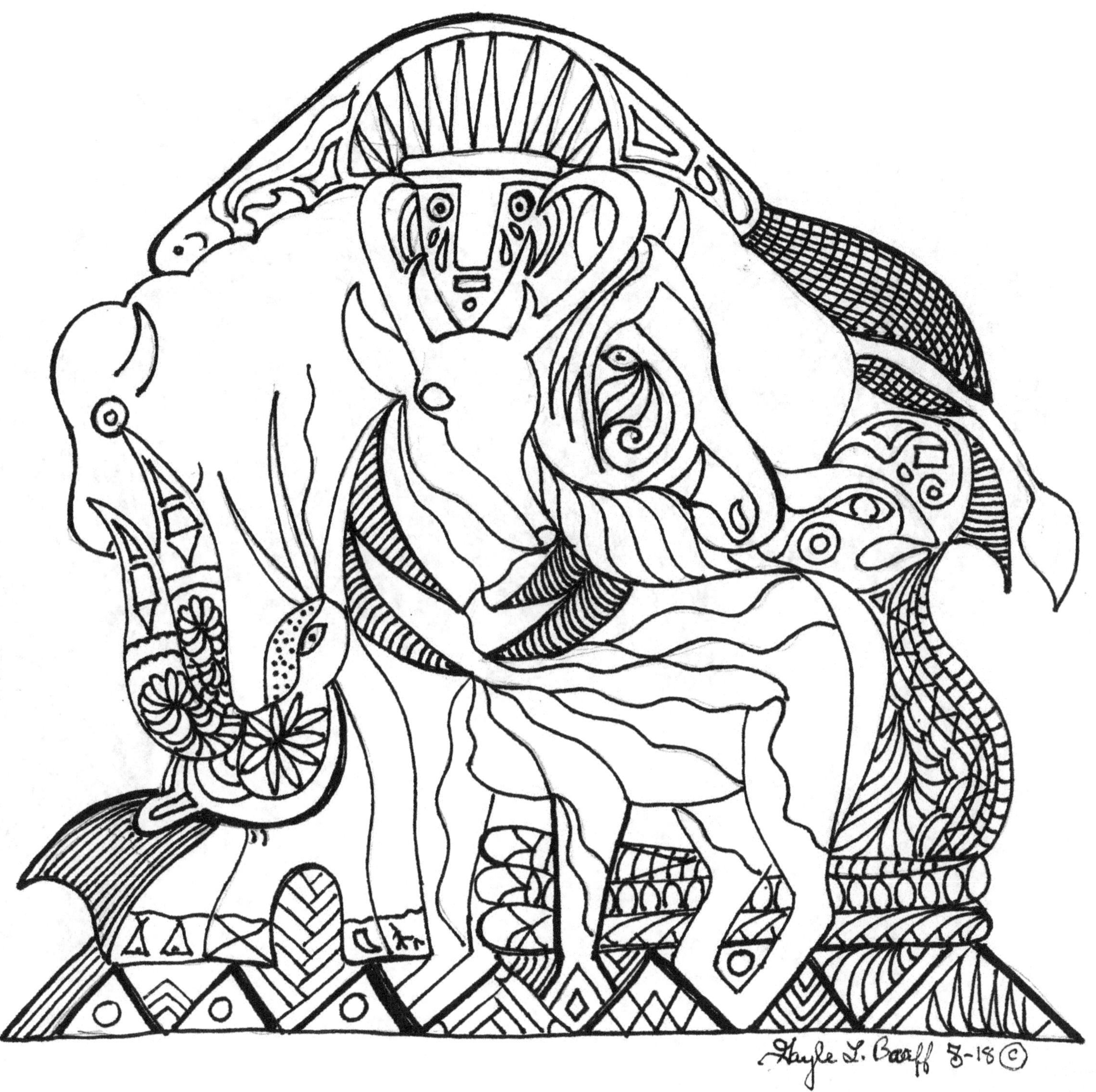

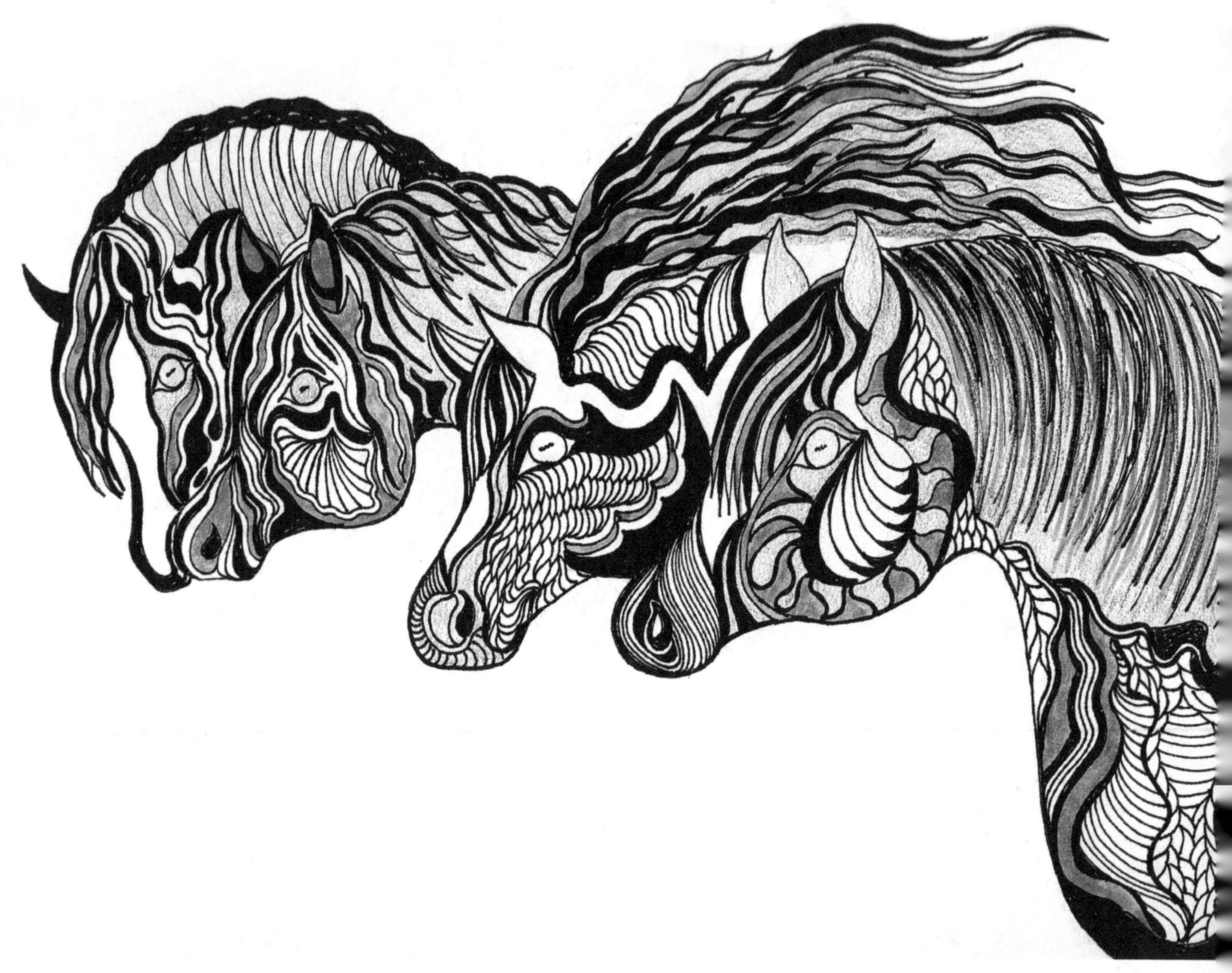

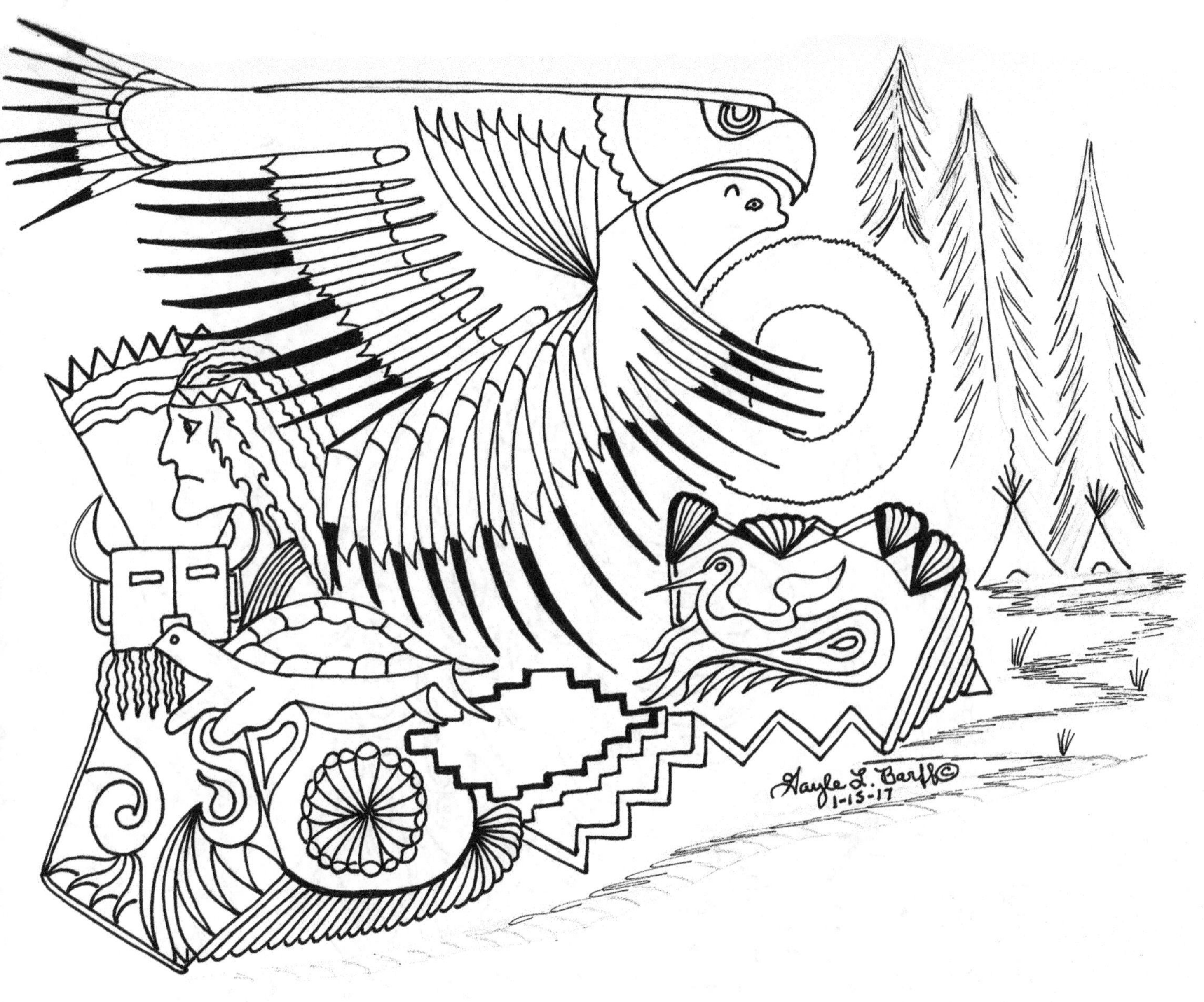

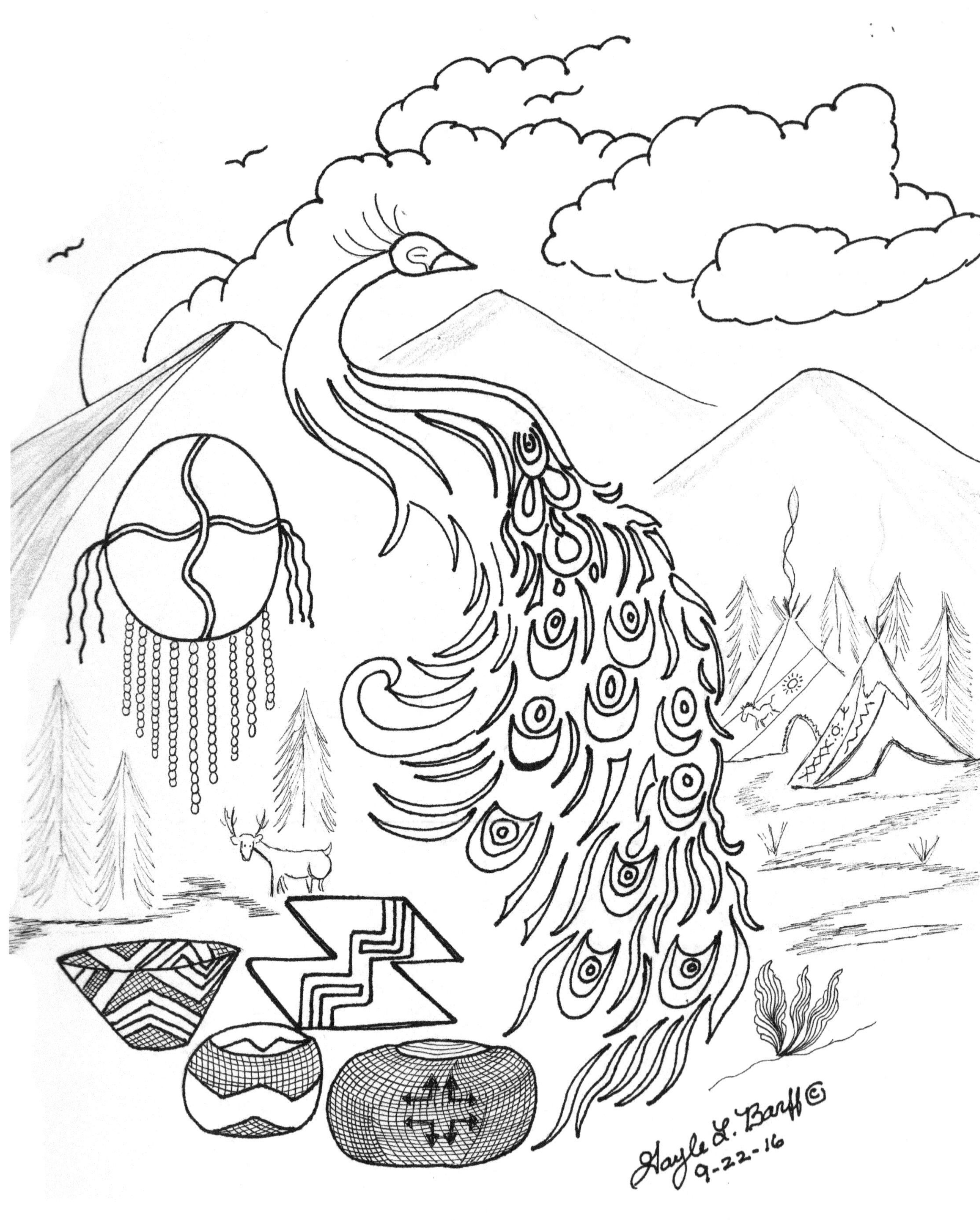

Gayle L. Barff ©
9-22-16

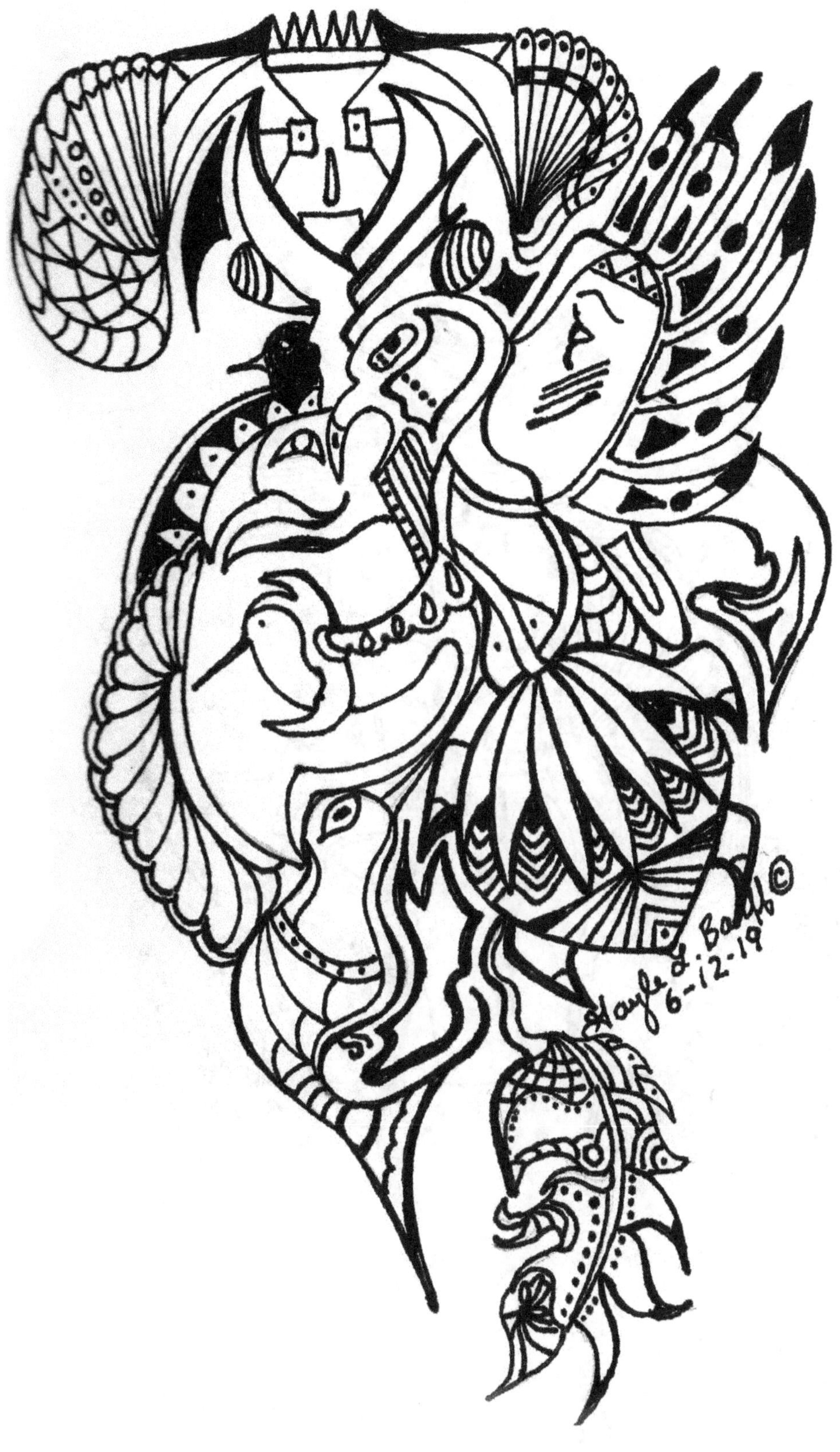

Gayle Barff

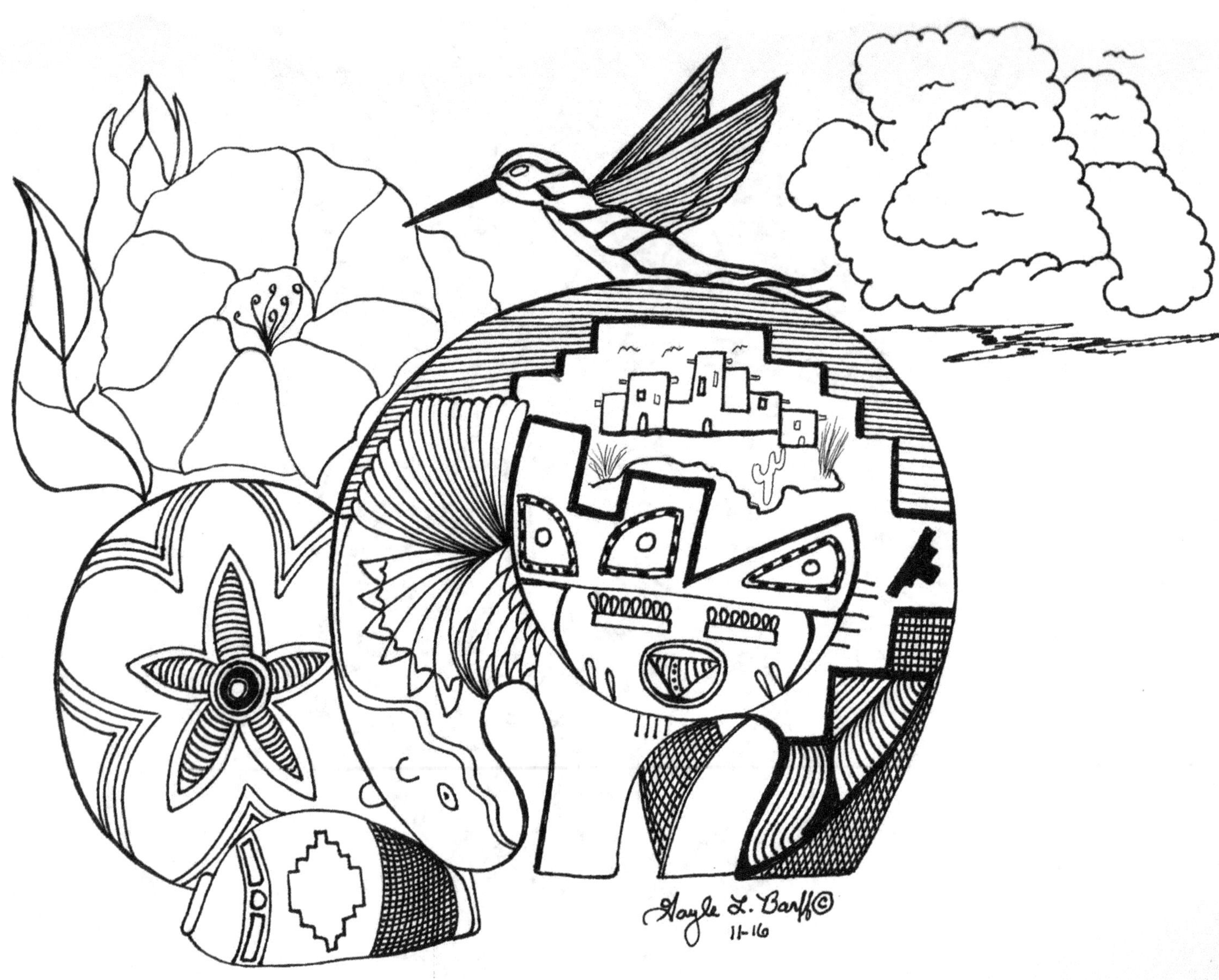

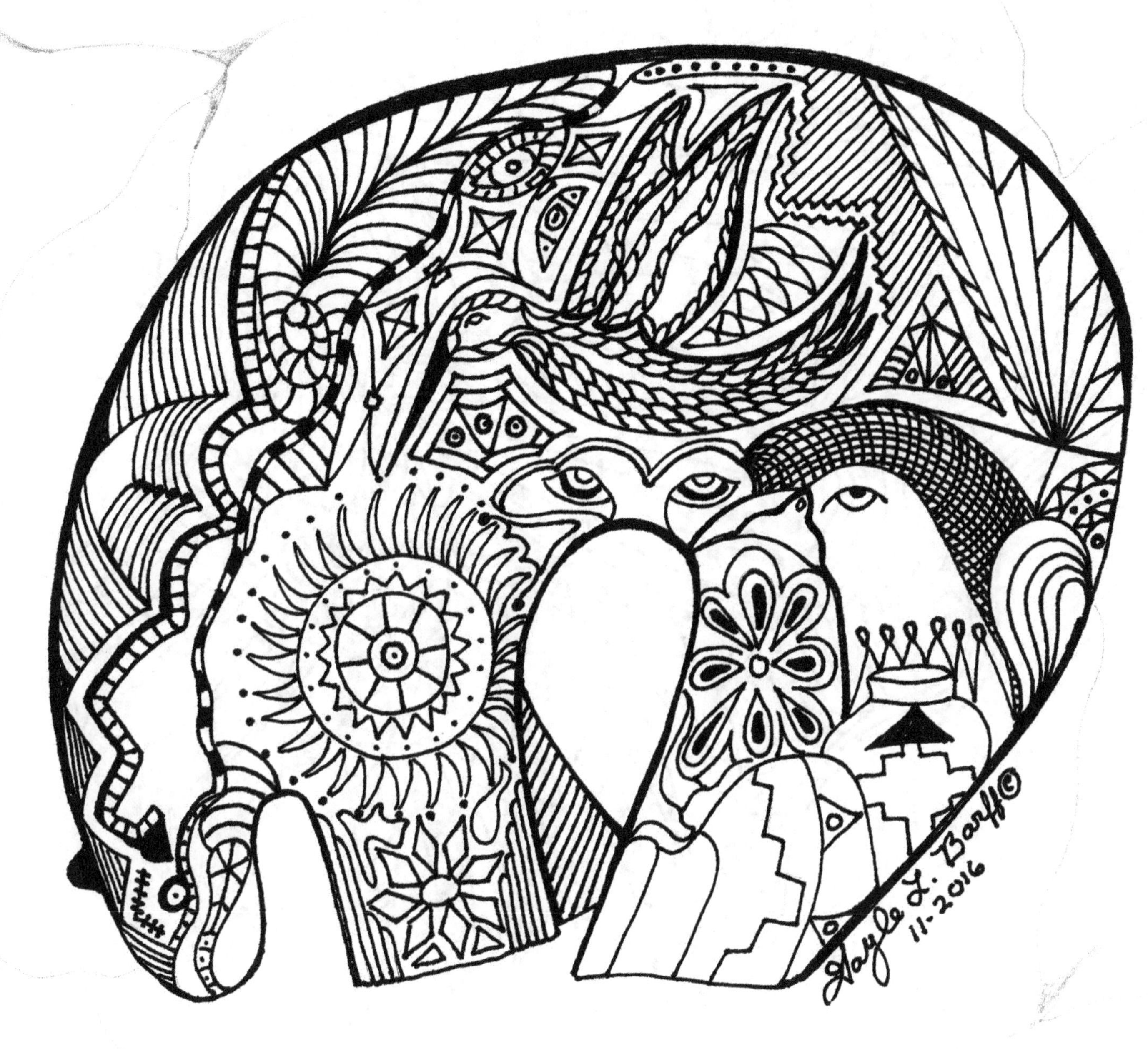

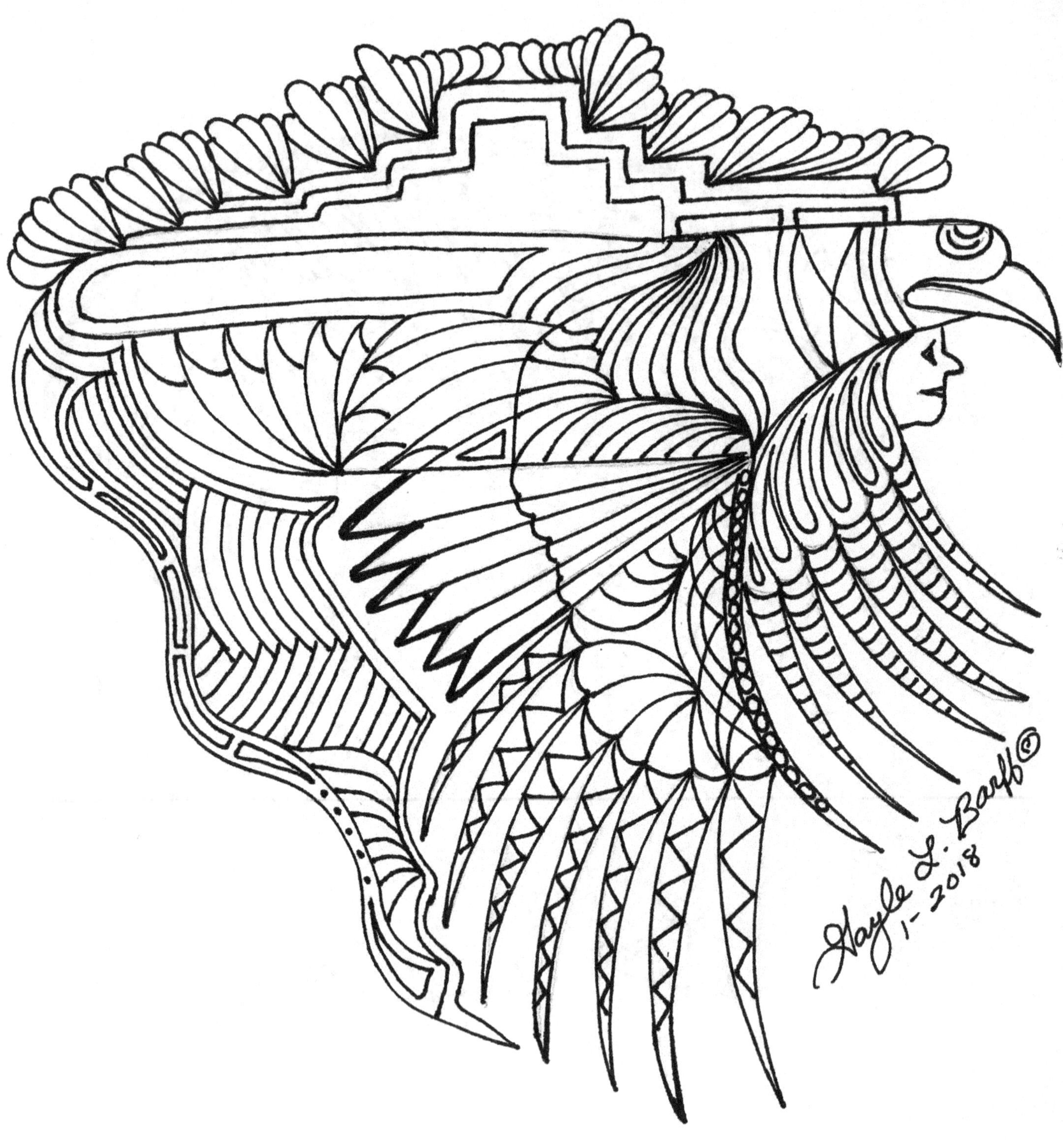

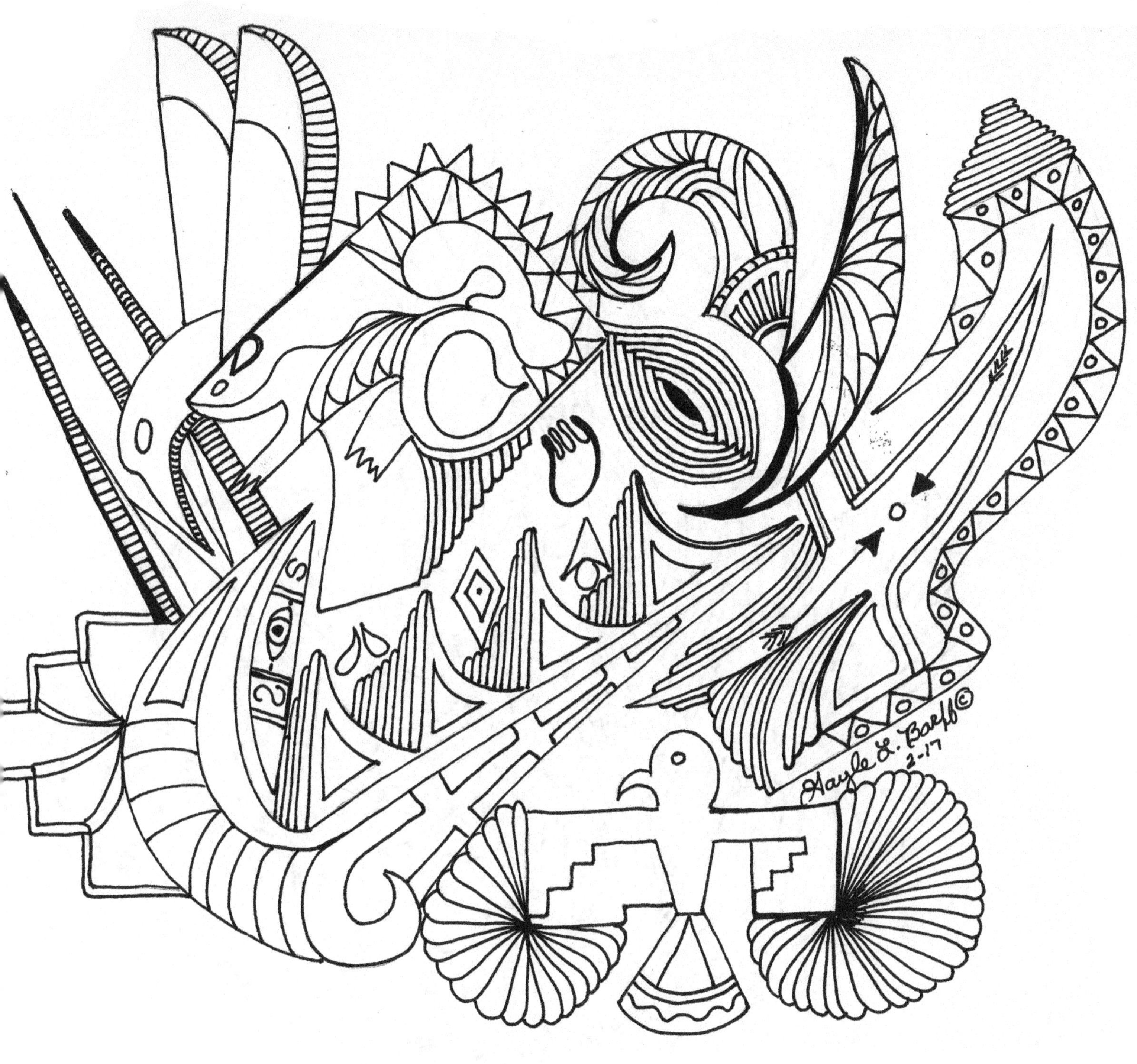

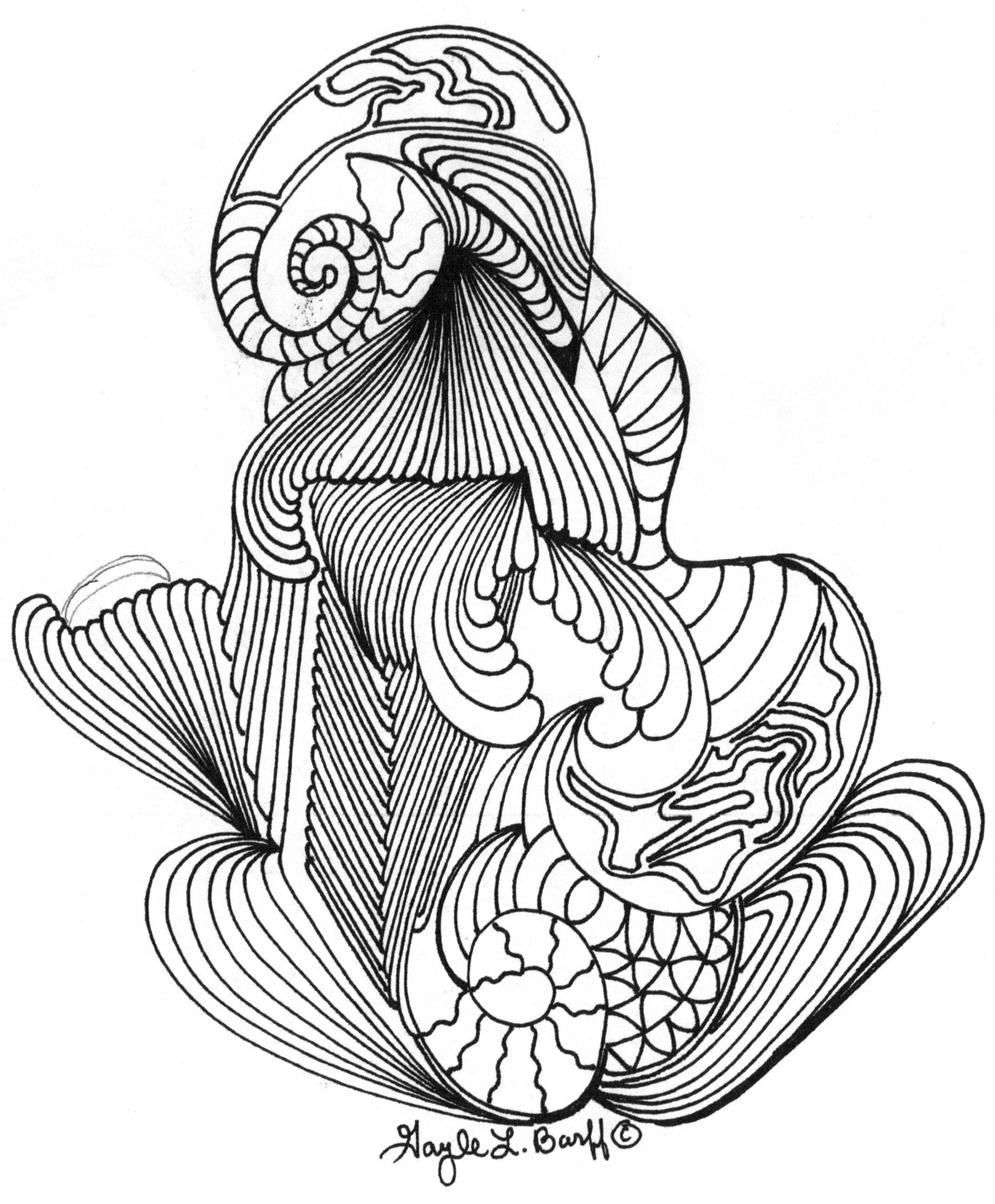

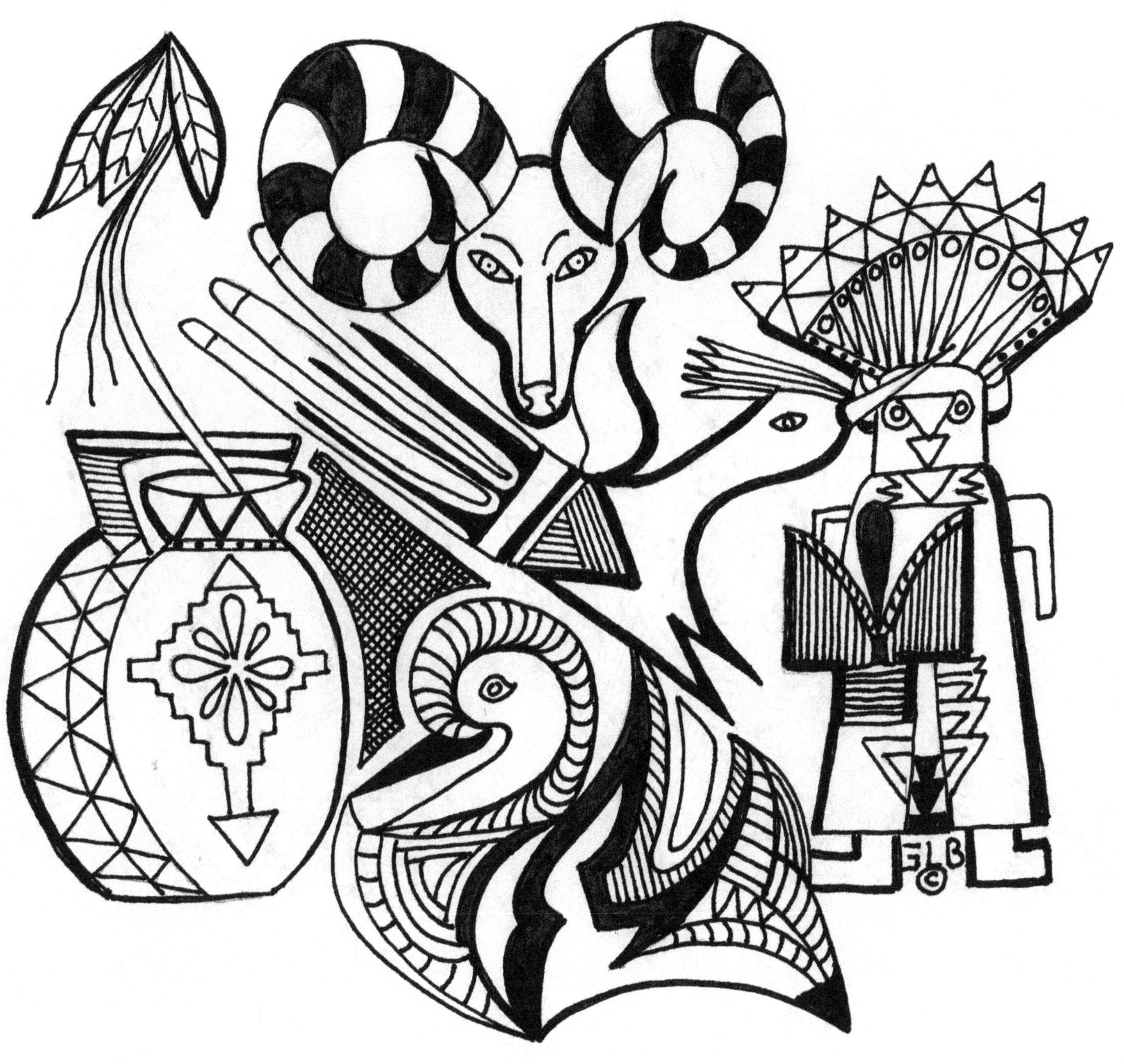

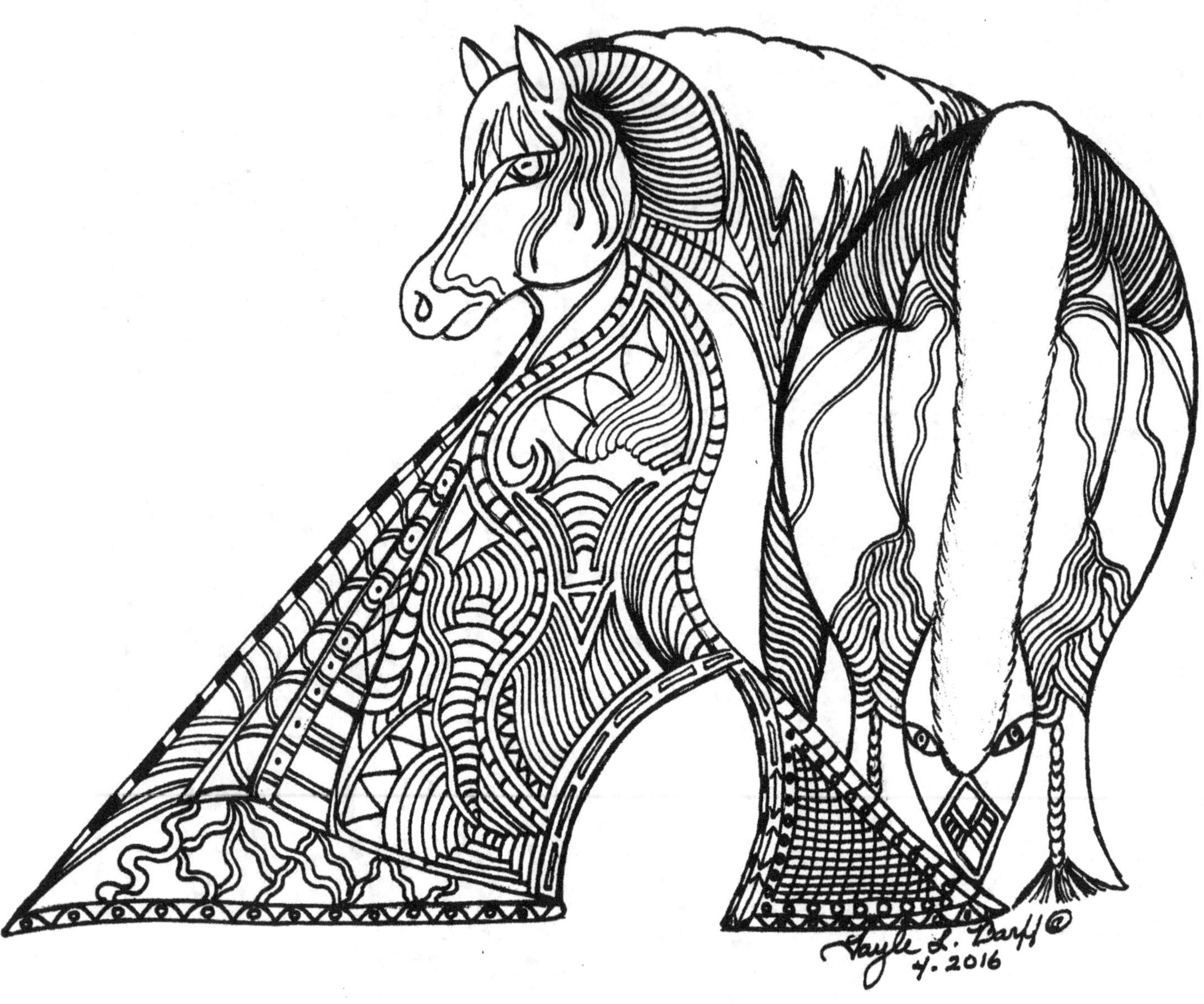

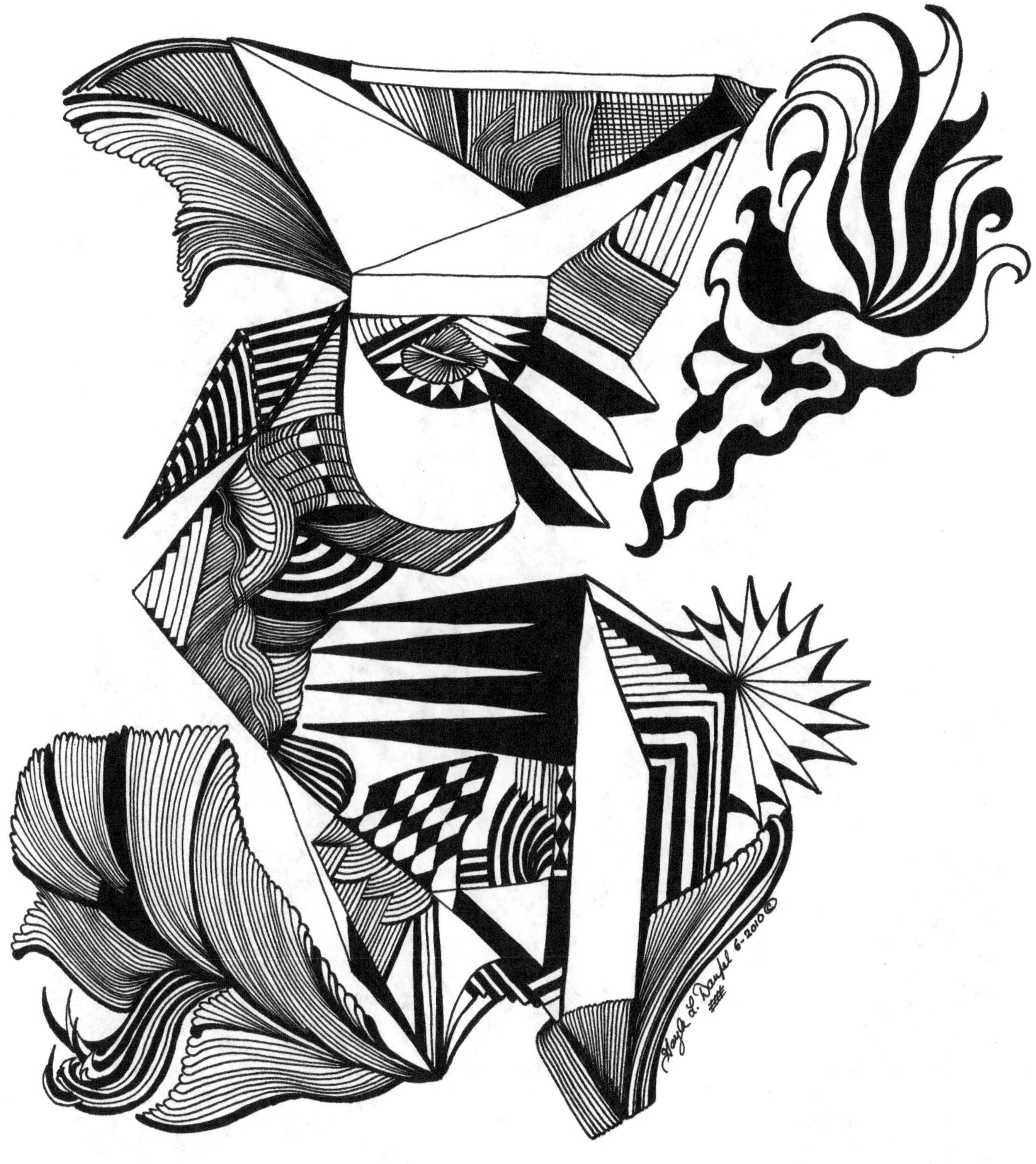

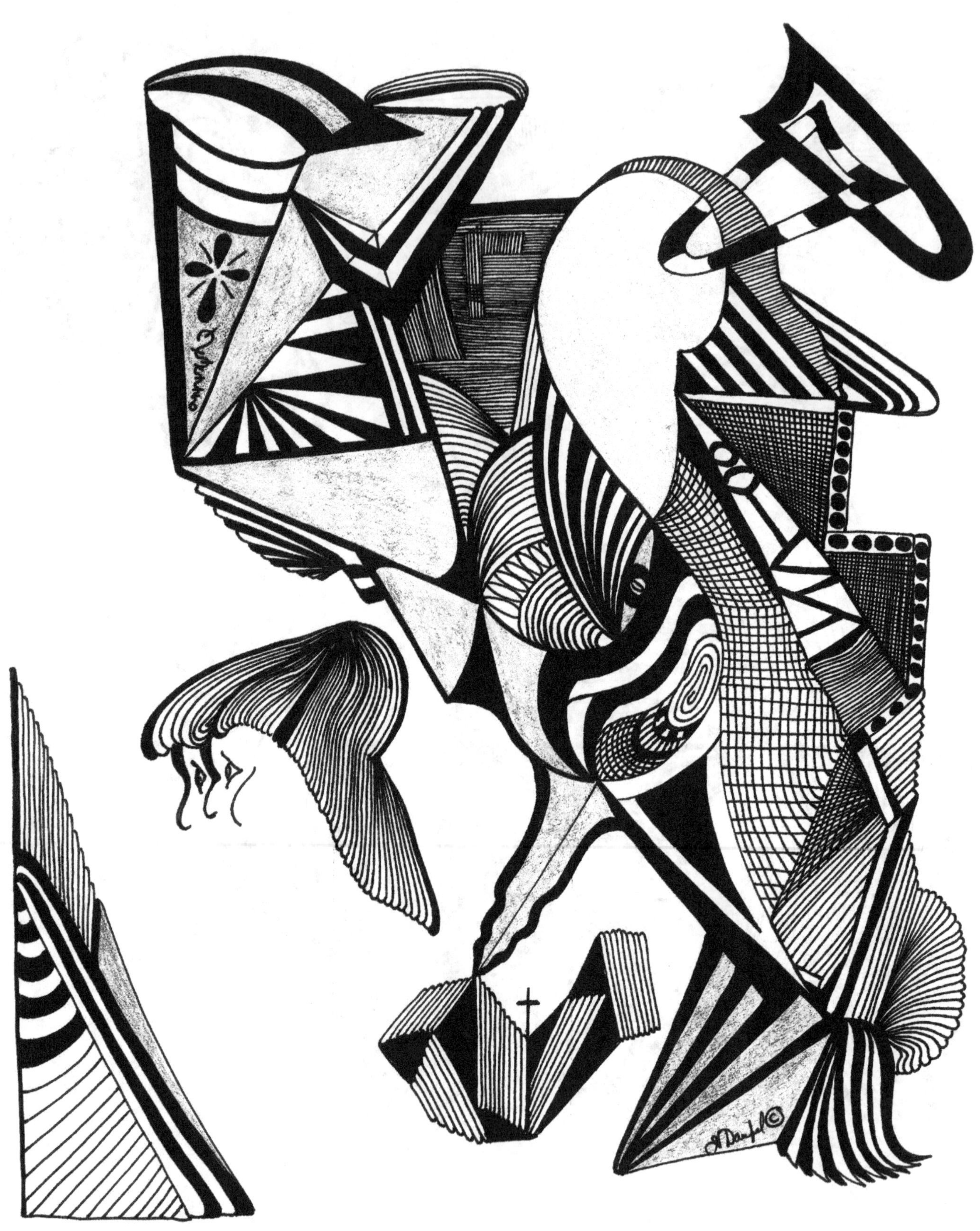

15

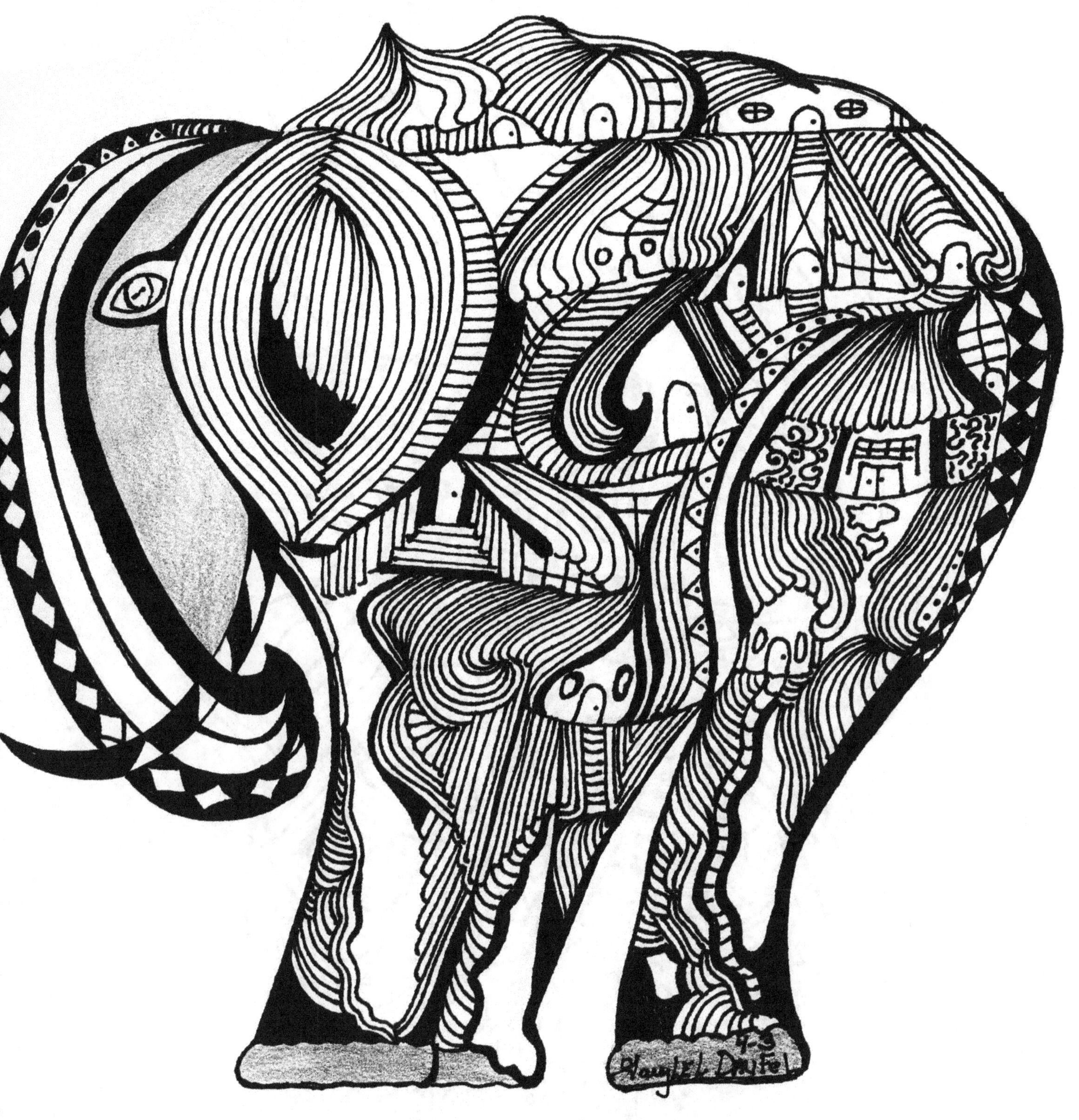

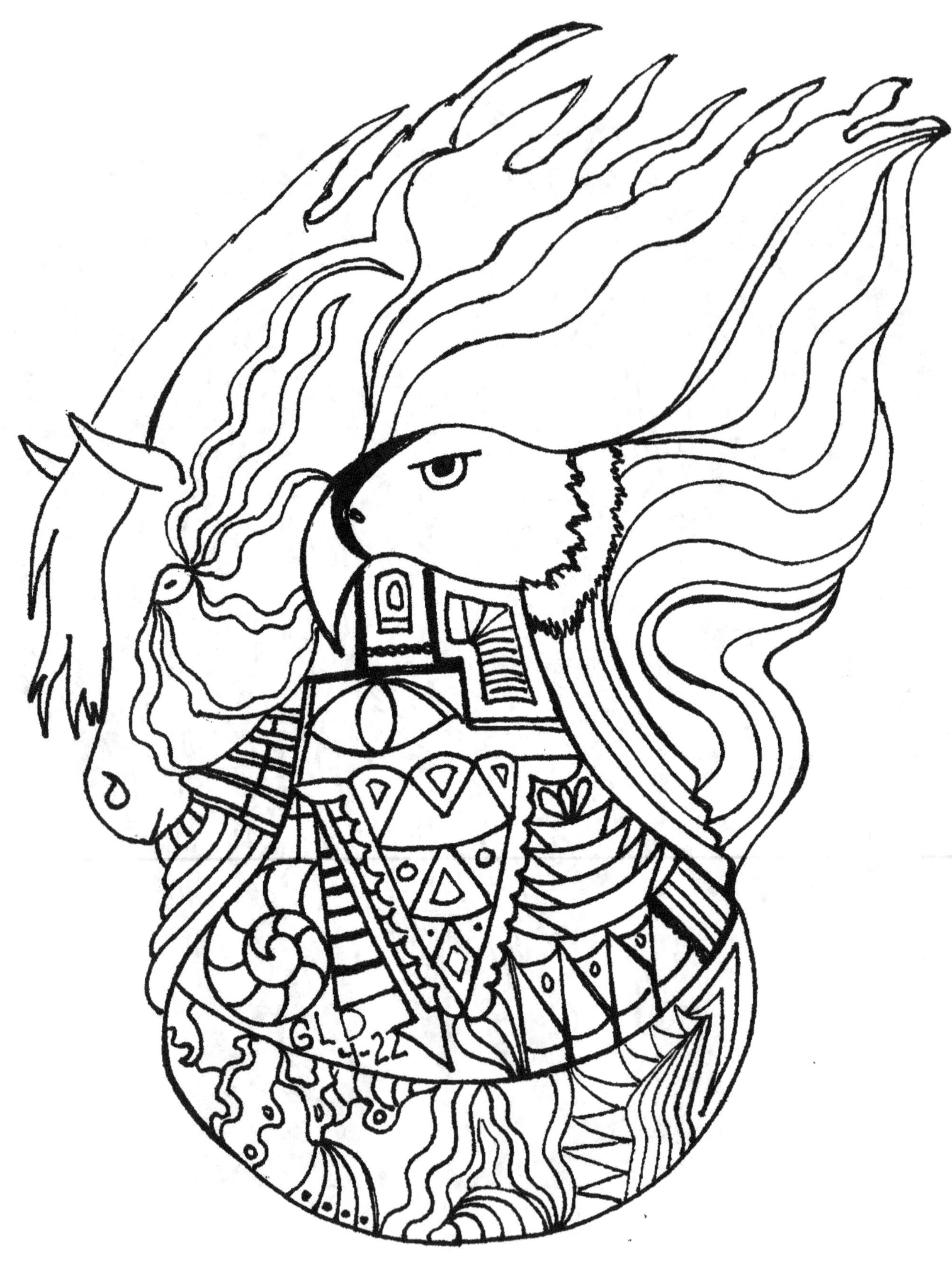

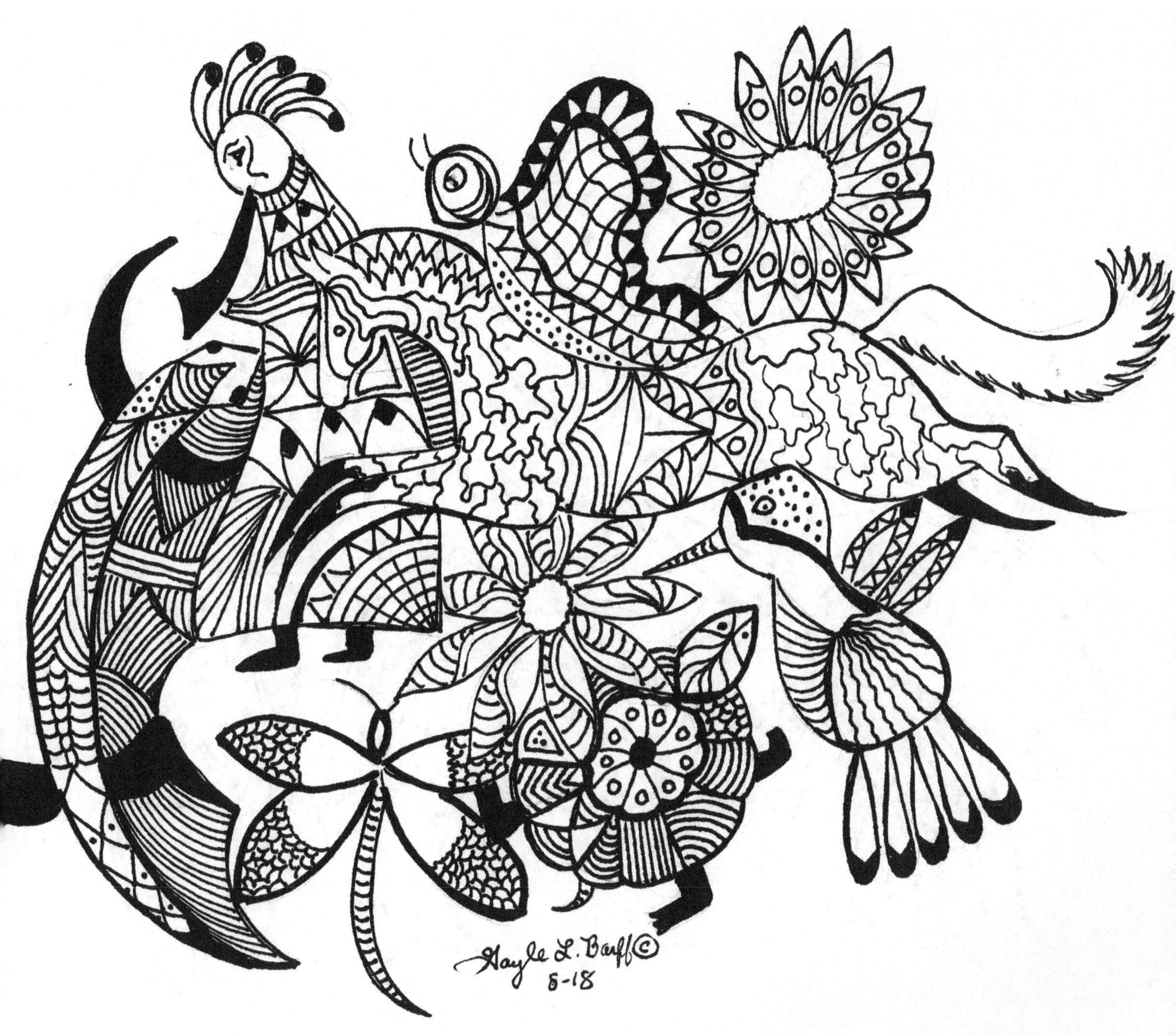

Gayle Barff

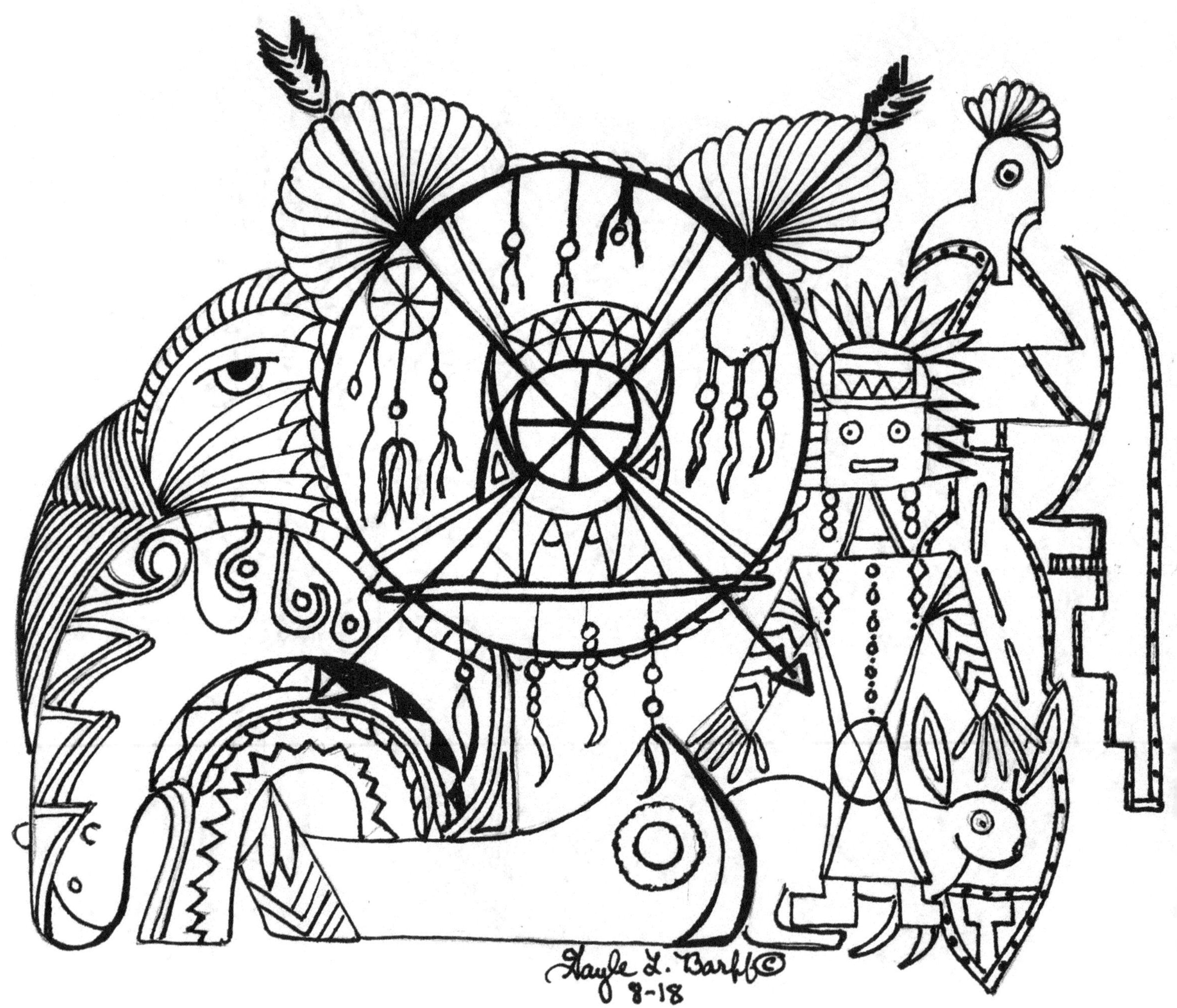

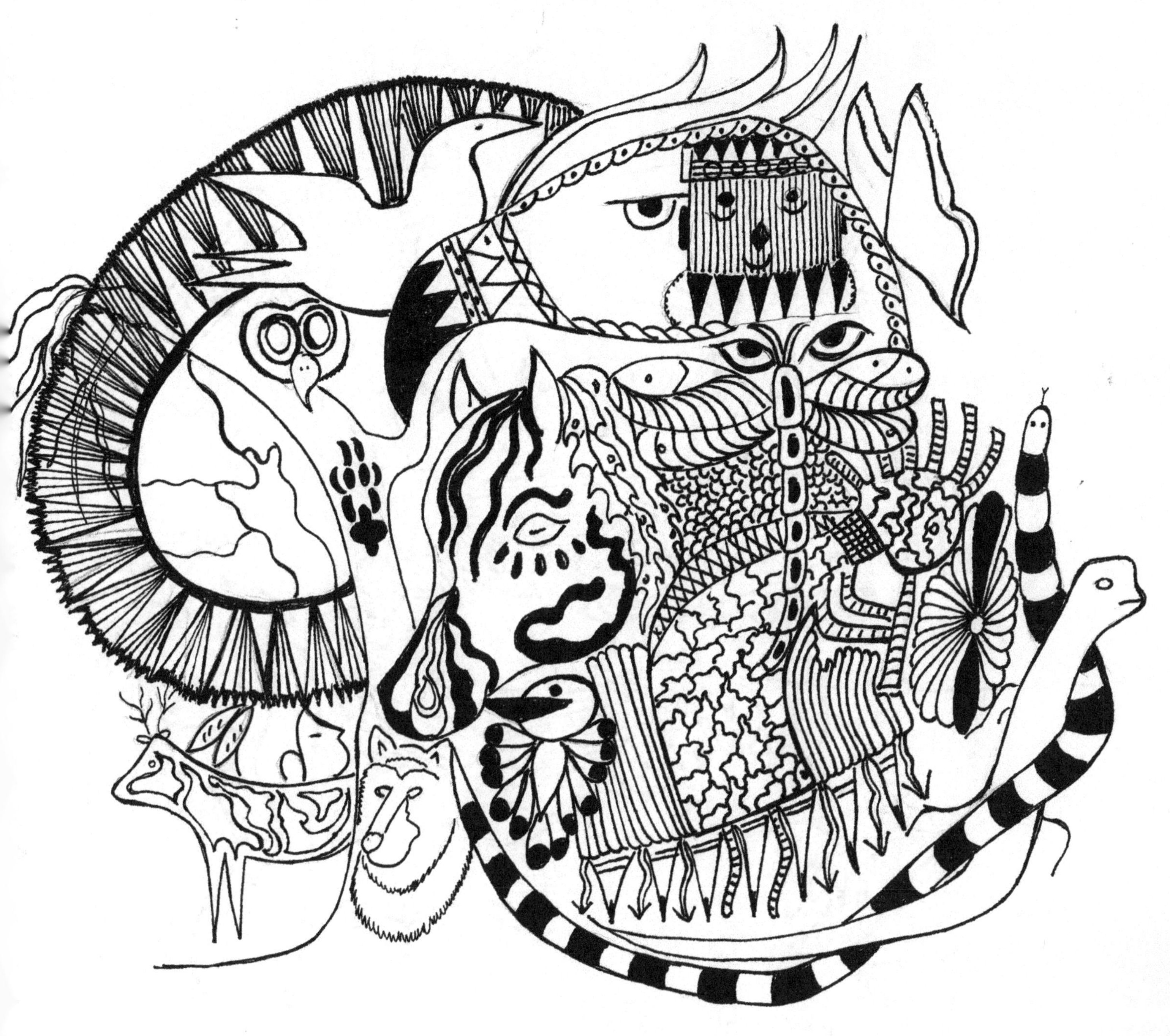

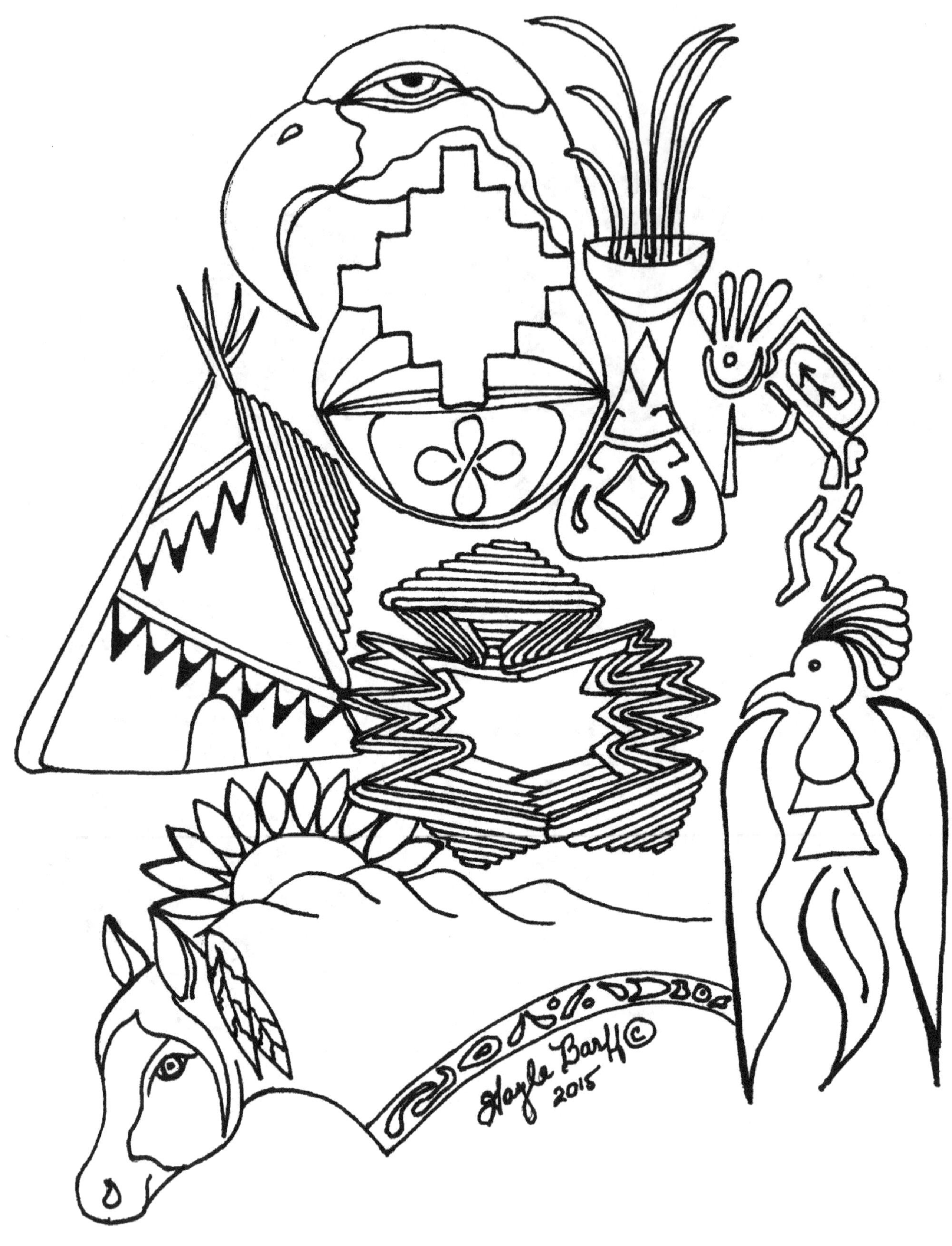

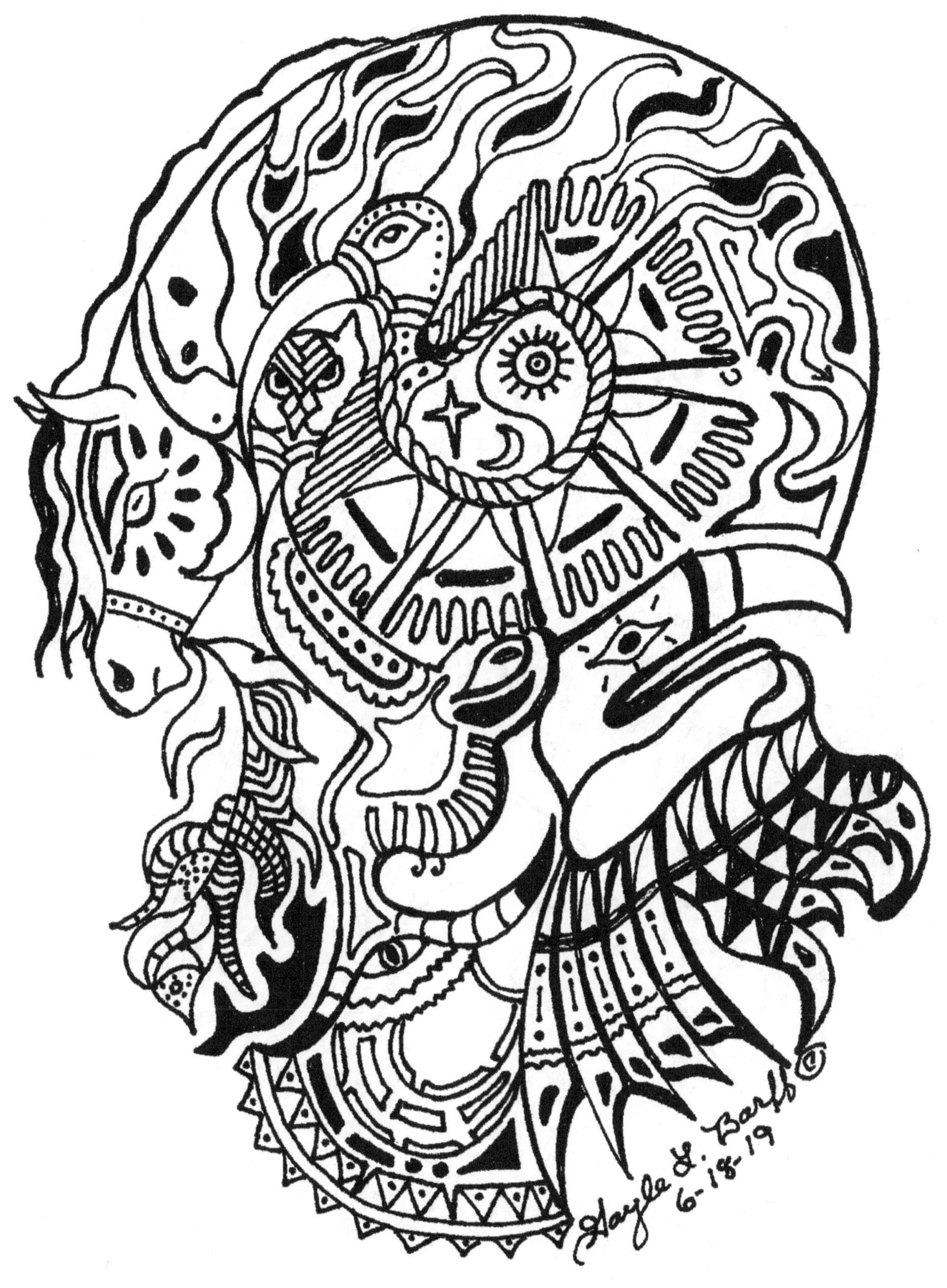

Gayle Y. Barff ©
6-18-19

Gayle Barff

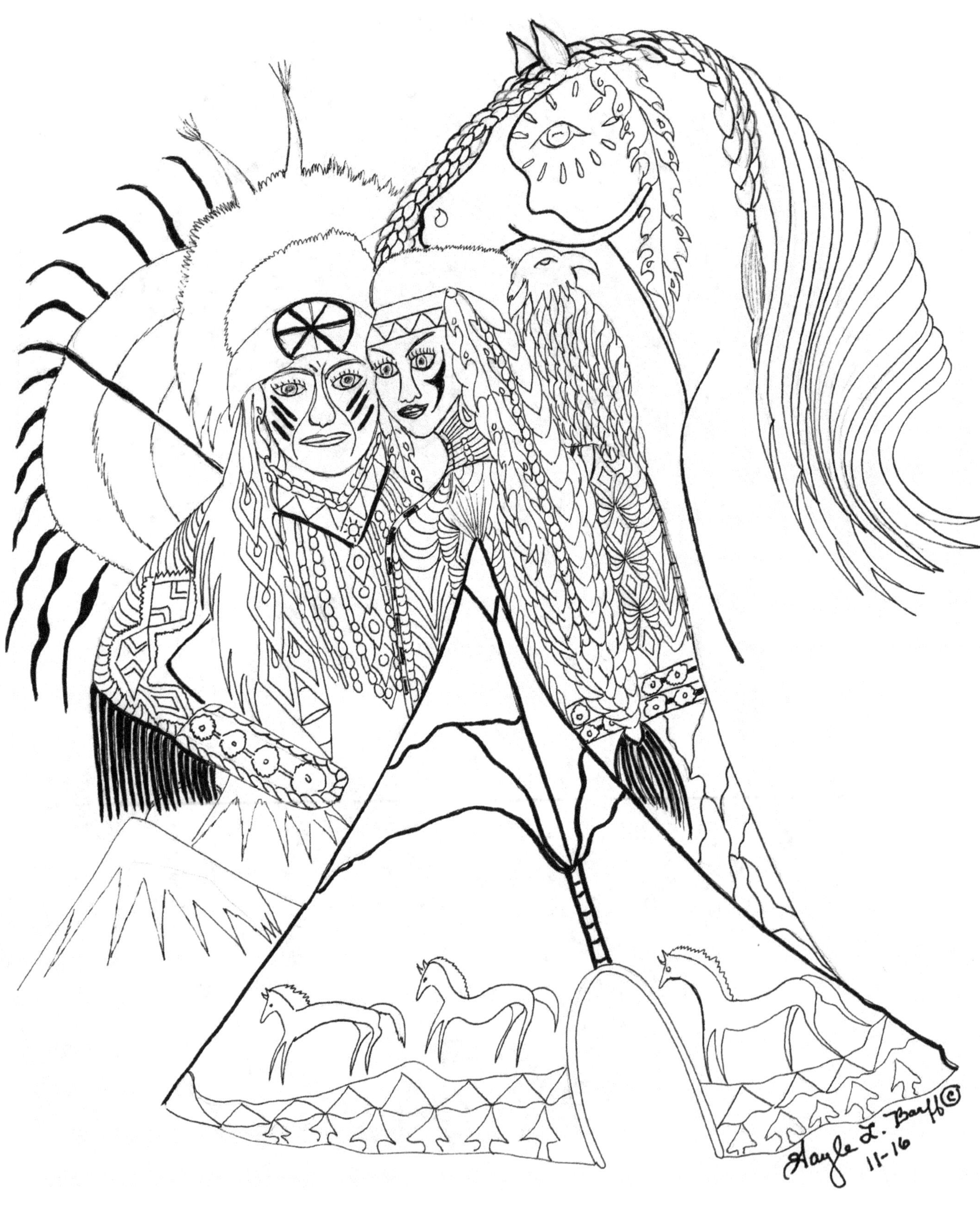

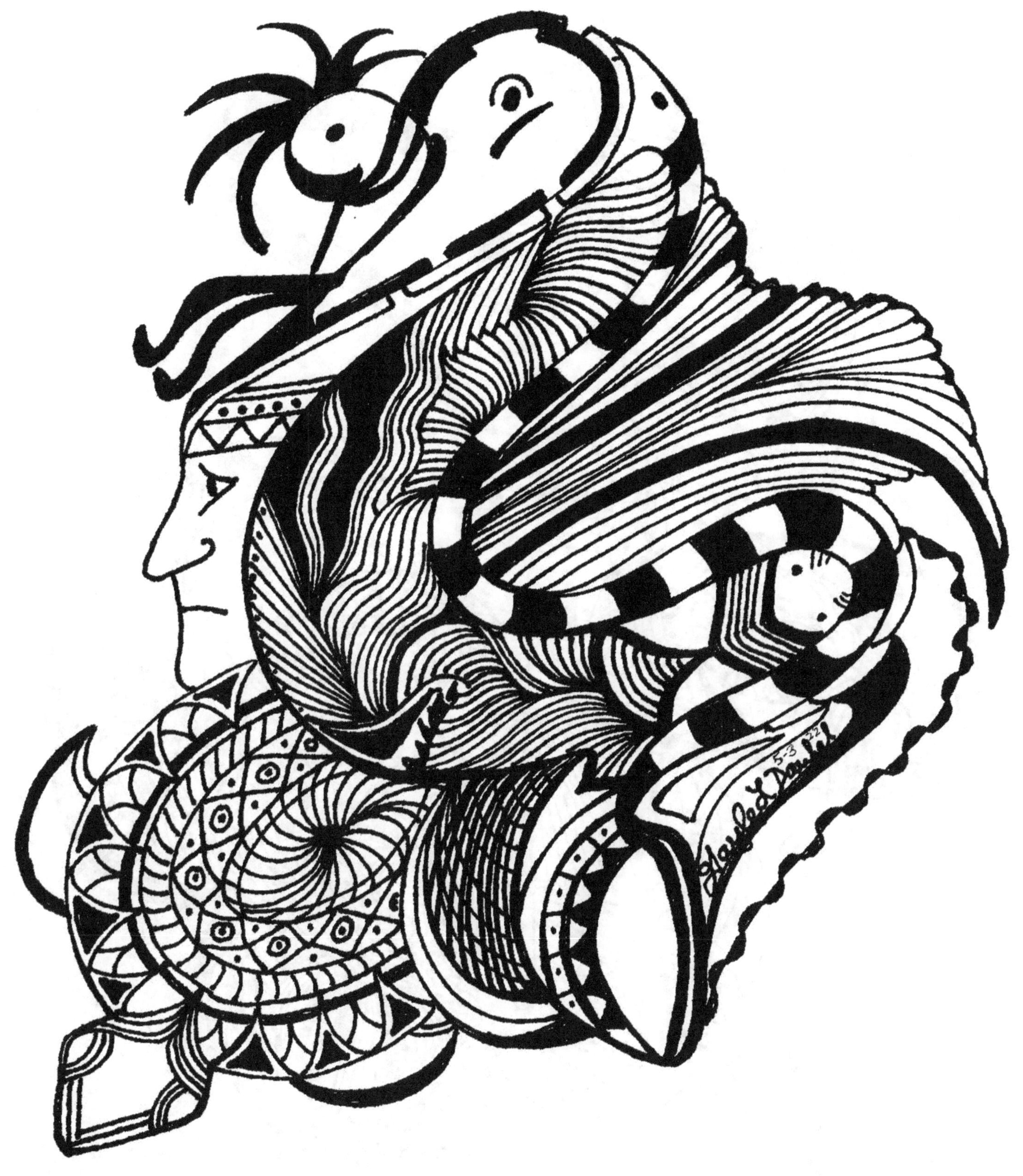

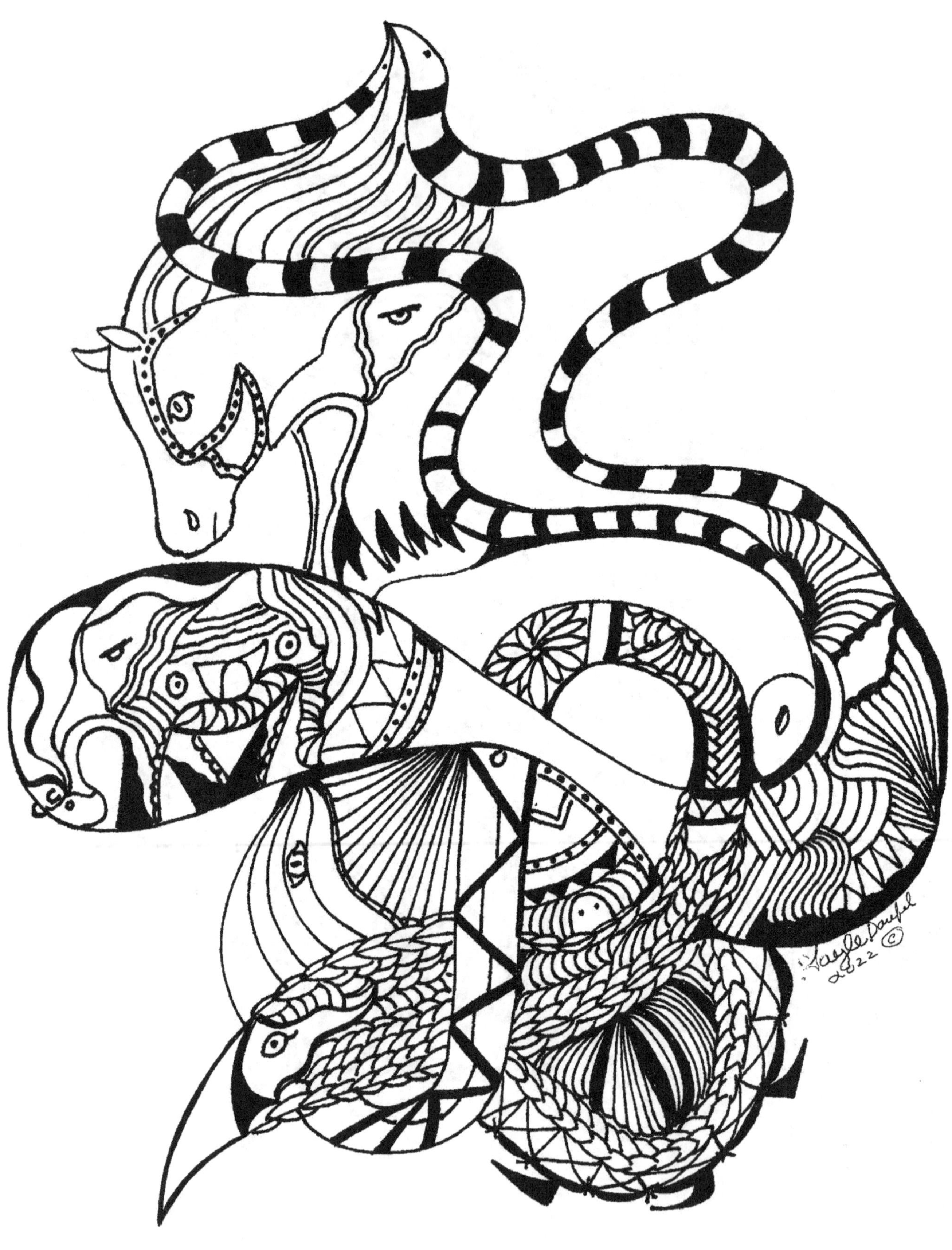

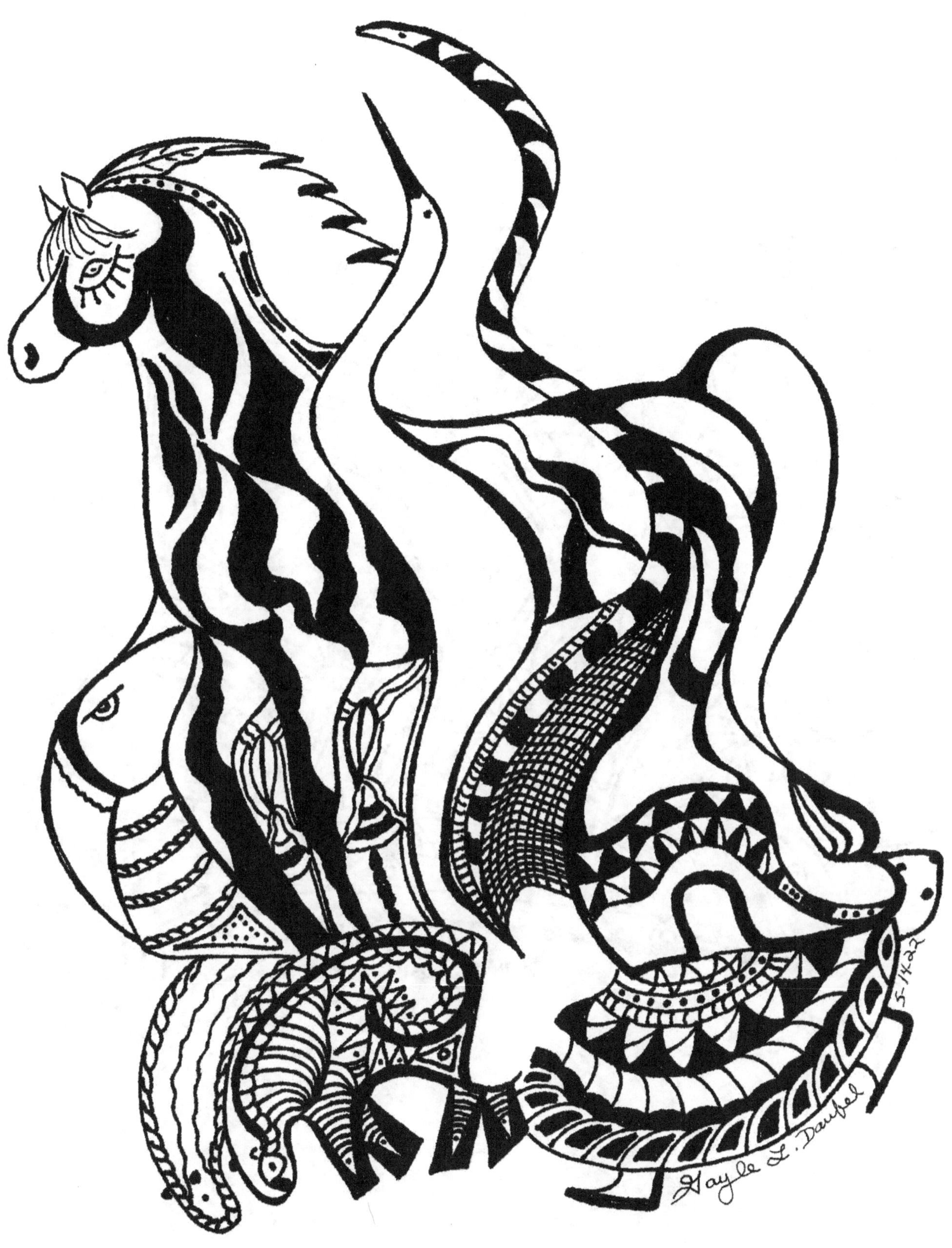

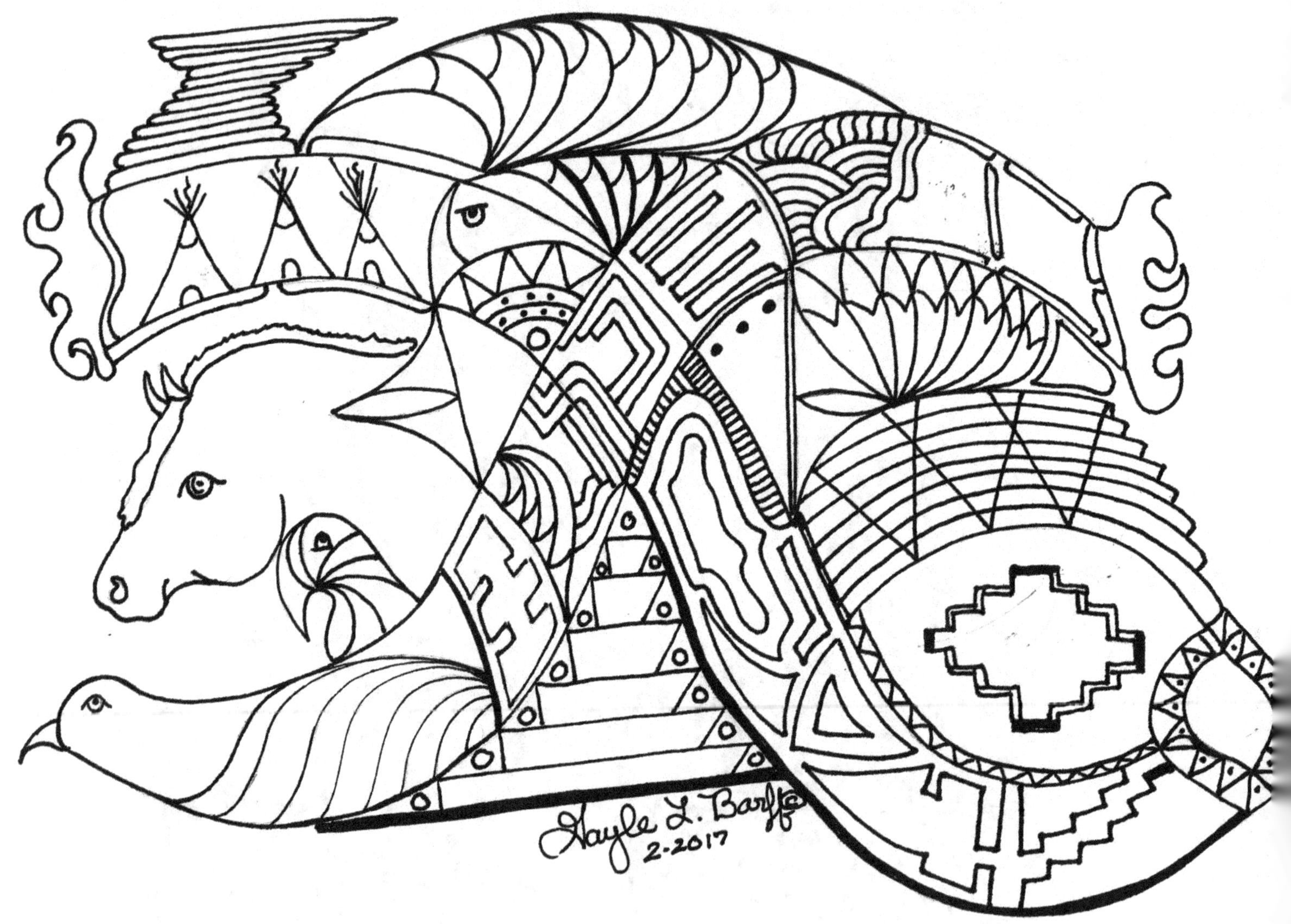

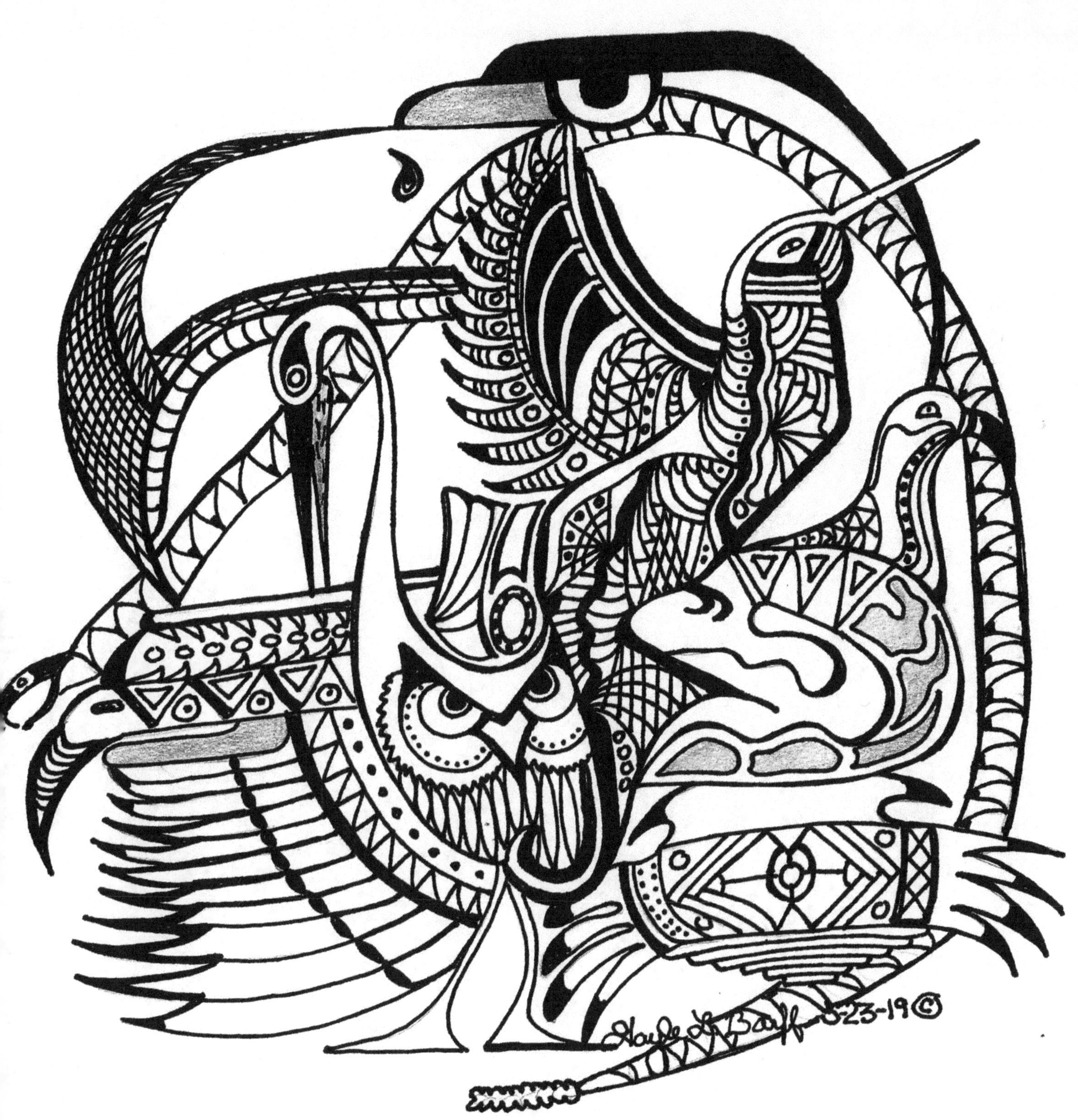